WHSmith

Practise

Spelling and
Grammar

KS2 ENGLISH

Age 7–9

Brenda Stones

Advice for parents

Most parents find there's some basic bit of spelling or grammar they've forgotten: this book is intended to lay a firm foundation in both skills for the early years of Key Stage 2.

What's unusual about this book is that it links spelling to grammar.

- The book starts with hearing the sounds of familiar words, moves on to practise accurate spelling of the vowel sounds and the consonants, and then explains which parts of speech you're dealing with.
- It also gives children techniques for collecting groups of words, so that they begin to enjoy discovering the patterns in spelling and grammar.
- In this way your child will gain basic confidence in using words – while also becoming aware of the many variations in the English language.
- It is probably advisable to tackle only one double page at a time, as there is plenty of content in each topic.

- The **'Get ready'** section provides a gentle warm-up for the topic covered in the unit.
- The **'Let's practise'** section is usually the main activity. This section helps to consolidate understanding of the topic. The questions in this section get progressively harder.
- The **'Have a go'** section is often a challenge or something interesting that you can go away and do which is related to the topic. It may require you to use everyday objects around the home.
- The **'How have I done?'** section at the end of the book is a short informal test that should be attempted when all the units have been completed. It is useful for spotting any gaps in knowledge, which can then be revisited at a suitable moment.
- Answers are supplied for right/wrong exercises, and the book ends with a poem.

First published 2007
exclusively for WHSmith by
Hodder Murray, a member of the Hodder Headline group
338 Euston Road
London
NW1 3BH

Impression number   10 9 8 7 6 5 4 3 2 1
Year   2008 2007
Text and illustrations © Hodder Education 2007

A CIP record for this book is available from the British Library.

Cover illustration: Sally Newton Illustrations
Character illustrations: Beehive Illustration
All other illustrations: Simon Dennett at SD Illustration, Arthur Pickering and Kelly Gray
Typeset by Florence Production Ltd, Stoodleigh, Devon

ISBN – 13   978 0 340 94539 1

Printed and bound in Scotland

Contents

Welcome to Kids Club!

Hi, readers. My name's Charlie and I run Kids Club with my friend Abbie. Kids Club is an after-school club which is very similar to one somewhere near you.

We'd love you to come and join our club and see what we get up to!

I'm Abbie. Let's meet the kids who will work with you on the activities in this book.

My name's Jamelia. I look forward to Kids Club every day. The sports and games are my favourites, especially on Kids Camp in the school holidays.

Hi, I'm Megan. I've made friends with all the kids at Kids Club. I like the outings and trips we go on the best.

Hello, my name's Kim. Kids Club is a great place to chill out after school. My best friend is Alfie – he's a bit naughty but he means well!

I'm Amina. I like to do my homework at Kids Club. Charlie and Abbie are always very helpful. We're like one big happy family.

Greetings, readers, my name's Alfie! Everybody knows me here. Come and join our club; we'll have a wicked time together!

Now you've met us all, tell us something about yourself.
All the kids filled in a '**Personal Profile**' when they joined. Here's one for you to complete.

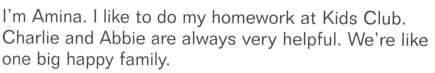

Personal Profile

Name: _____

Age: _____

School: _____

Home town: _____

Best friend: _____

My favourite:

● Book _____

● Film _____

● Food _____

● Sport _____

My hero is _____ because _____

_____

When I grow up I want to be a _____

If I ruled the world the first thing I would do is _____

_____

If I could be any celebrity for a day I would be _____

_____

1: Making plurals

You remember that **plural** means more than one: so a single **dog**, but plural **dogs**. Can you remember all the rules for making plurals?

Examples

1 For most words just add **s**: lots of **bugs** and lots of **bees**.
2 For words that end with **ss**, **sh**, **ch** or **x**, you need to add **es**, to help you say the word: one **fox**, but lots of **foxes**.
3 For words that end in **o**, you usually add **es**: one **flamingo**, lots of **flamingoes**.
4 For words that end in **y**, you change the ending to **ies**: one **fly**, lots of **flies**. But if there's a vowel before the **y**, you just add **s**: one **monkey**, lots of **monkeys**.
5 For words that end in single **f** or **fe**, you usually change the ending to **ves**: one **calf**, lots of **calves**.
6 And then there are irregular plurals, which you just have to learn, like **men**, **women** and **children**.

Get ready

When the animals entered Noah's ark, there were:

Two _____

Two _____

Two _____

Two _____

Let's practise

1. One bunch, lots of _____
2. One box, lots of _____
3. One volcano, many _____
4. One dish, stacks of _____
5. One potato, heaps of _____
6. One mess, masses of _____
7. One dinosaur, two _____
8. One envelope, bags of _____
9. One class, several _____
10. One glove, a pair of _____

11. One fairy, lots of _____
12. One dwarf, lots of _____
13. One diary, bags of _____
14. One child, a class of _____
15. One donkey, six _____
16. One man, a crowd of _____
17. One cowboy, two _____
18. One knife, several _____
19. One jelly, lots of _____
20. One calf, a herd of _____

Have a go

Now can you think of **collective nouns** to describe these plural things?

A _herd_ of buffaloes

A _____ of bees

A _____ of birds

A _____ of dolphins

2: Building words

It always helps your spelling if you can break down words into their separate parts, especially with **root words** and **compound words**.

Examples

1   These are all **root words**, with endings or beginnings built on:
   From **happy** you can build **unhappy**, **happiness** and **happily**.
   From **walk** you can build **walking** and **walker**.
   From **child** you can build **childish** and **childlike**.

2   These are all **compound words**, with two separate words added together:
   foot + ball = football
   tooth + brush = toothbrush
   light + house = lighthouse

Write a sentence using words built from the root word **play**.

_____

_____

_____

Let's practise

Root words

1. What is the root word for **jumping** and **jumped**? _____

2. What is the root word for **quicker** and **quickest**? _____

3. What is the root word for **hopeful** and **hopeless**? _____

4. What is the root word for **washable** and **washing**? _____

5. What is the root word for **dislike** and **likeness**? _____

Compound words

6. green + house = _____

7. air + port = _____

8. play + ground = _____

9. hair + cut = _____

10. card + board = _____

11. sauce + _____ = _____

12. _____ + shine = _____

13. _____ + cup = _____

14. eye + _____ = _____

15. toe + _____ = _____

Have a go

How many things that are **compound words** can you find in the kitchen?

_____

_____

3: Prefixes and suffixes

This is really about building words again.

If you add to the *beginning* of the word it's called a **prefix**.

And if you add to the *end* of a word it's called a **suffix**.

Examples

Prefixes on the front

1   **un-** makes these words mean 'not': **unhappy**, **unwise**, **unusual**.
2   **pre-** makes these words mean 'before': **prepare**, **prehistoric**.
3   **re-** makes these words mean 'again': **repeat**, **restart**, **regain**.

Suffixes on the end

1   **-ful** makes these words mean 'full of': **hopeful**, **fruitful**.
2   **-less** makes these words mean 'without': **hopeless**, **meaningless**.
3   **-able** makes these words mean 'able to': **workable**, **drinkable**.

How many more words beginning with **un-** can you think of?

You could use your dictionary to make a list.

_____

_____

_____

Let's practise

Fill in all the boxes.

1 Prefixes

Prefix	Root word	New word	Meaning
un	able	unable	cannot do
		uncommon	
	true		
		unusual	
	even		
pre	historic		
		preview	
re	fresh		
		refund	
	cycle		

2 Suffixes

Root word	Suffix	New word	Meaning
pain	ful	painful	hurts a lot
		powerful	
meaning			
		plateful	
	less		no pain
spot			no spots!
life	less		
walk	able		
		bearable	
		suitable	

Have a go

Use words with suffixes to complete these sentences.

On a good day I feel _____

On a bad day I feel _____

4: Silent letters

I've heard about **silent letters**. You can't hear them when you say the word, but they're in the spelling because of old English words.

Examples

1   Silent **g** in words like **gnome** and **gnash**.
2   Silent **k** in words like **knee** and **know**.
3   Silent **w** in words like **write** and **wring**.
4   Also silent **w** in the question words **who** and **whose**.
5   And usually silent **h** in the question words **what**, **why**, **when**, **where** and **which**.

Fill in all the boxes.

If you want to find out	You ask
The date or time	When?
The reason	
The place	
Which person	
	Whose?
	What?
	Which?

Let's practise

Fill in all the spellings and meanings.

Silent letter	Spelling	Meaning
w	wreck	old ship
	wrist	
		very small bird
		not right
	wrinkle	
k	knock	
		man in armour
	knit	
	knife	
g	gnarled	
	gnaw	

Have a go

Write a short questionnaire to find out people's earliest memories.
Use each of the question words (in any order) from the table opposite.

1 _____

2 _____

3 _____

4 _____

5 _____

6 _____

7 _____

I remember the five vowels are **a**, **e**, **i**, **o**, **u**. But when do they make short vowel sounds, and when do they make long vowel sounds?

Examples

1 The **short vowel sounds** are as in the words
bag, **beg**, **big**, **bog**, **bug**.

2 The **long vowel sounds** are as in the words
bay, **bee**, **by**, **boat**, **boot**.
It usually takes two vowels to spell a long vowel sound.
The long vowel sound **a** can be spelt like r**ai**n or d**ay**.
The long vowel sound **e** can be spelt like b**ea**n or f**ee**l.
The long vowel sound **i** can be spelt like m**y** or d**ie**.
The long vowel sound **o** can be spelt like c**oa**t or gr**ow**n.
The long vowel sound **u** can be spelt like m**oo**n or gr**ew**.

3 Then there's **magic e**: when you add this **e** to the end of a word with a short vowel sound, it changes the sound to a long vowel sound.
mat becomes **mate**   **not** becomes **note**
pet becomes **Pete**   **cut** becomes **cute**
pin becomes **pine**

Get ready

Say the words aloud as you fill in all the boxes.

Short vowel	Add magic e	Short vowel	Add magic e
fin	fine		hope
spit		dam	
	fate	bit	
cub			shine
mop			robe
	cane	spin	

Let's practise

Put these words in the right pot for short vowel sounds, long vowel sounds from pairs of vowels, or long vowel sounds with magic **e**.

hit	moon	bank	feet	phone	plate	pun	fond
fin	lie	stay	moan	line		fate	pole

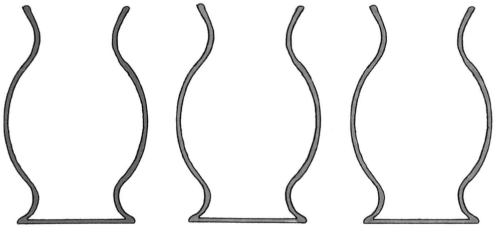

Short vowel sounds   Long vowel sounds   Magic **e**

Fill in rhyming words to complete the poem.

To run is f_____

To race is a_____

To shine is f_____

To care is r_____

6: Endings after short vowels

If I want to add an ending beginning with a vowel, like **-ing** or **-ed**, to a word like **frost** or **flop**, what's the problem?

Examples

1   **frost** and **frosting**
    If the word has a **short vowel sound** and ends with **two consonants**, you just add the ending.
    thump and **thumping**, **lump** and **lumped**

2   **flop** and **flopping**
    If the word has a **short vowel sound** and ends with just **one consonant**, you have to *double the last consonant* to keep the vowel sound short.
    fit and **fitter**, **hit** and **hitting**

Fill in rhyming words with short vowel sounds.

bat	met	fin	hot	mug
ch____	b____	sh____	pl____	b____
th____	g____	ch____	sh____	h____
fl____	l____	th____	bl____	pl____

Add endings to words with short vowel sounds.
Watch your spelling!

Short vowel word	Add -ing	Add -ed	Add -er
flip	flipping	flipped	flipper
stop			
fold			
pat			
pop			
ban			
slip			
pot			
mist			
chat			
thin			

Have a go

Single or double consonants?
Check whether the vowel
sound is short or long, and
then you can decide.

Fill in all the boxes.

Short vowel	Long vowel
tinny	tiny
	diner
matting	
	pining
	fusing
	mated
fatted	
	striped

I like these: it's actually easier to add endings to words with long vowel sounds than short vowel sounds.

Examples

1 If the word has a **long vowel sound** and ends with a **consonant**, just add the ending, like **sleet**, **sleeting** or **sleety**.
2 If the word ends with **magic e**, take off the **e** and add the ending, like **make** and **making**.
3 If the word ends with either **y** or **ie**, like **fry** or **die**:
   put a **y** before **-ing**, like **frying** and **dying**;
   put an **i** before **-ed**, like **fried** and **died**.

Fill in all the boxes.

Root word	-ing ending	-ed ending
fry	frying	fried
try		
cry		
die	dying	died
lie		
tie		

Let's practise

Fill in all the boxes.

Root word	-ing ending	-y ending	-ed ending
squeak	squeaking	squeaky	squeaked
float			
brood			
sneak			
	raining		
		needy	
flake			flaked
	posing		
		stony	
phone			phoned
taste	tasting		tasted
bone			
paste		pasty	

Have a go

Don't forget that there are other long vowel sounds made by pairs of letters. Can you add more examples?

1 **ar** as in *spark*, _____

2 **aw** as in *bawdy*, _____

3 **oi** as in *moist*, _____

4 **ou** as in *house*, _____

5 **ow** as in *rowdy*, _____

8: Words with -le endings

Do you know how to spell words that end with an 'ul' sound?

Usually you spell them **-le**, like **jungle** and **riffle** and **rifle**.

Examples

1   The easiest spellings are words with a **short vowel sound** followed by **two consonants** before **-le**: like **crumple** and **uncle**.

2   If there's a **short vowel sound** and **one consonant sound** before **-le**, you *double the last consonant*, as in Unit 6. Fill in all these.

-ttle	-ddle	-zzle	-bble	-ffle
li_____	pu_____	dri_____	bu_____	ra_____
bo_____	mu_____	pu_____	pe_____	ski_____
ski_____	mi_____	fi_____	dri_____	shu_____

3   If there's a **long vowel sound**, you only need one consonant before **-le**. (Decide which consonant you need to complete these words.)

t*a*ble	**ea**gle	st*i*fle	r*u*ble
ca_____	trea_____	Bi_____	bu_____
fa_____	peo_____	ri_____	doo_____
sta_____	nee_____	tri_____	poo_____

Get ready

Rain poem
Fill the gaps with **-le** words from this page.

In the mi_____ of the dri_____,
While we're sh_____ling through the pu_____s,
Let's keep blowing bu_____s
Till the dri_____ is a dri_____.

Let's practise

Put these **-le** words in the right pots:

muffle	jumble	dawdle	jungle	piffle	giggle
juggle	scramble	marble	bauble	trickle	cradle

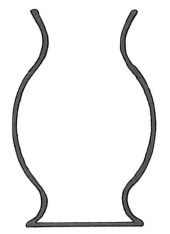
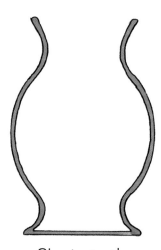
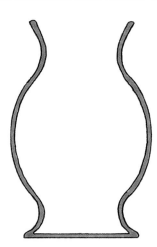

Short vowel followed by two consonants

Short vowel followed by a double consonant

Long vowel sound

Annoyingly, there are some exceptions to the **-le** spelling.

Can you fill in this grid with more words?

-al ending	-el ending
final	easel
tribal	label
legal	hazel

9: The frightful spelling *gh*

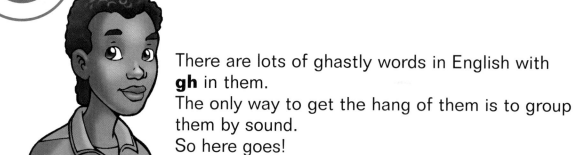

There are lots of ghastly words in English with **gh** in them.
The only way to get the hang of them is to group them by sound.
So here goes!

Examples

1   The easy one is **ight** as in **right**, **night** and **fight**.
2   The tricky one is **ough**, because it can be said so many different ways.
3   And then there are **augh**, **eigh** and **aight**, which you just have to learn!

Let's take them slowly, one by one.

Get ready

These are all spelt with **ight**. Fill in the words, then write their meanings.

1   br_____   meaning _____

2   f_____   meaning _____

3   fl_____   meaning _____

4   fr_____   meaning _____

5   kn_____   meaning _____

6   l_____   meaning _____

7   n_____   meaning _____

8   r_____   meaning _____

9   s_____   meaning _____

10 t_____   meaning _____

Let's practise

Now for the dreaded **ough** words.
At least these are all spelt the same.

Put them under the headings of how
they are said:

plough	although	bought	drought	fought	sought
borough	enough	nought	rough	trough	dough

'ow(t)' sound	'off' sound	'oh' sound	'oo' sound	'ort' sound	'uh' sound	'uff' sound
bough	cough	though	through	thought	thorough	tough

Have a go

And finally the words with terrible spellings like **augh**, **eigh** and **aight**,
which sound quite different from how they're spelt!

Put them under the headings of
how they are said:

sleigh	slaughter	straight
caught	daughter	weight

'arf' sound	'ay(t)' sound	'ite' sound	'ort' sound
laugh	eight	height	naughty

10: Endings: -able and -tion

I always get confused with words that end with **-able** or **-ible**.

It's so unfair! And then there are words ending **-tion** or **-sion** . . .

Examples

1   Words ending with **-able** include **portable** and **walkable**.
2   Words ending with **-ible** include **edible** and **audible**.
3   Words ending with **-tion** include **station** and **nation**.
4   Words ending with **-sion** include **tension** and **pension**.

And the reason behind their spelling is just the groups of Latin words they happen to come from.

Invent a household robot, using as many **-able** words as you can.

Describe what you'd expect of it.

_____

_____

_____

Let's practise

Fill in these words.

① **-able** endings

Can be printed: p_____

Can be relied on: r_____

Can be read: r_____

Worth a lot: v_____

② **-ible** endings

Can be eaten: e_____

Can be bent: fl_____

Can be read: l_____

Can be seen: v_____

③ **-tion** endings

Text under a picture: c_____

A feeling: e_____

A book that isn't fact: f_____

A choice: op_____

④ **-sion** endings

A sum: div_____

Money when you retire: p_____

A large house: m_____

What you do before tests: rev_____

Have a go

Can you list some of the words that end with **-ssion**?

mission, passion, _____

And any words that end with **-shion**? _____

_____

11: Apostrophes

Do you know what an **apostrophe** is, and when we use it?
It's a flying comma like this **'**, and it has two quite separate uses: first to show a missing letter, and second to show ownership.

Examples

1   Missing letters
    I am can be written **I'm** if we cut out the **a**.
    He is can be written **He's** if we cut out the **i**.
    It is can be written **It's** if we cut out the **i**.

2   Only one owner
    If a car has only one driver, we say the
    driver's car. If there's *only one owner*, the
    apostrophe goes *before* the **s**.

3   Lots of owners
    If a car has lots of drivers, we say the
    drivers' car. If there are *lots of owners*,
    the apostrophe goes *after* the **s**.

Get ready

Fill in all the boxes.

Full	Short	Cut
she is	she's	i
I have		
we had		
	we're	
	they've	
do not		
cannot		
	it's	
	who's	
should not		
must not		

Let's practise

Remember, it all depends on how many owners. Rewrite the following with apostrophes.

1   One queen has one crown.
    The queen's crown

2   One queen has lots of crowns. _____

3   Two queens have two crowns. _____

4   Two boys share one football. _____

5   One camel has two humps. _____

6   One soldier has one leg. _____

7   Two grannies share one house. _____

8   Two grannies own two houses. _____

Have a go

If the plural doesn't end with **s**, you still put the apostrophe after the owners, but before the **s**: the **men's story** and the **women's story**.

Write in apostrophes where they are needed here:

9   The childrens legs

10   The childrens toy

11   The mens trousers

12   The ladies shoes

Shall I tell you about **homonyms** first?
They are words that are *spelt the same*, but have *different meanings*.
So I **wave** my hand, or there's a **wave** in the sea.

Then I'll tell you about **homophones**.
They are words that *sound the same* but have *different spellings*, because they have different meanings.
So I **hear** that you're **here**.

Examples

1 The word **homonym** comes from *homo* meaning 'same' and *nym* meaning 'name'.
   Same name: I can fill in a **form**, or look at the **form** of my drawing.
2 The word **homophone** comes from *homo* meaning 'same' and *phone* meaning 'sound'.
   Same sound: We **write** the **right** thing down.

Get ready

Make up sentences to show the meaning of these **homonyms**:

1 (swallow – the bird / swallow – when you eat)

_____

2 (mint – a green plant / mint – lots of money)

_____

3 (beat – to beat in games / beat – a stroke in music)

_____

4 (check – to make sure / check – squares)

_____

5 (rose – a flower / rose – got up)

_____

(Did you notice that homonyms are often different parts of speech?)

Read each sentence, check what the two words mean, then fill in the right **homophone**.

6 I _____ like to know which _____ you mean. (wood/would)

7 Let's make our _____ with a _____ of cake. (piece/peace)

8 I _____ you had _____ socks on. (new/knew)

9 _____ way did the _____ go? (witch/which)

10 _____ saying that they live _____. (they're/there)

11 I think the _____ will take _____ time. (sum/some)

12 I reckon _____ pieces is _____ few. (too/two)

13 _____ doubt you _____ the answer. (no/know)

14 This _____ is a _____ lot harder to dig. (whole/hole)

15 _____ did you _____ this coat before? (wear/where)

Have a go

Its and **it's** are one of the hardest homophones.
It's always means **it is** or **it has**, so test whether you can say **it is** or **it has** instead. **Its** is always possessive. (The cat sat on **its** tail.)
Fill in the right spelling.

16 I know that _____ not always easy to know if _____ right.

17 But _____ meaning should be as clear as _____ always been.

18 _____ just a question of checking what _____ meant to mean.

19 On _____ own, _____ never a problem.

20 But _____ right to feel perplexed about how _____ used.

13: Adjectives

I know what **adjectives** are! They're words that *describe* things, like **sunny** and **rosy**. Adjectives can make our writing more interesting.

Examples

He was a **big**, **ugly**, **bad-tempered** giant.
He lived in a **huge**, **damp**, **mouldy** cave.

Try thinking of an adjective for every letter of the alphabet.

My cat can be angry, bossy, cuddly, _____

_____

Get ready

Make a list of **adjectives** for each of the following:

1 My favourite holiday place is _____

2 My favourite food is _____

3 My favourite shoes are _____

4 My worst subject at school is _____

5 My favourite singer is _____

6 My favourite pet is _____

7 My worst weather is _____

8 My best friend is _____

9 My worst enemy is _____

10 My favourite book is _____

Let's practise

If we want to say that the giant is **bigger** or the **biggest**, we call these **comparative** and **superlative** adjectives.

Remember your spelling rules for adding suffixes, especially for short vowel sounds.

Fill in all the boxes.

Adjective	Comparative	Superlative
dark	darker	darkest
deep		
plain		
pale	paler	
stale		
tasty	tastier	
red		
dim		
thin		thinnest
fit		
batty		

Have a go

Make adjectives out of these nouns.

Each new adjective should have a different ending, or suffix.

Noun	Adjective
rose	rosy
friend	
book	
care	

31

I know about **synonyms**: they are words that have *similar meanings*.

And I know about **antonyms**: they are words with *opposite meanings*.

Examples

1   **Synonyms**
    Similar words to **dark** are **murky**, **dingy**, **gloomy**.
    Similar words to **wet** are **soaking**, **sopping**, **dripping**.

2   **Antonyms**
    The opposite of **happy** is **sad**, **mournful** or **morose**.
    The opposite of **smooth** is **bumpy**, **rocky** or **jagged**.

Get ready

Antonyms can be made by using prefixes or suffixes, as we did in Unit 3.
Fill in all the antonyms here:

Prefix	Root word	Suffix	Antonym
un	happy		unhappy
un	clear		
de	frost		
dis	agree		
dis	trust		
dis	honest		
im	possible		
im	polite		
	hope	less	
	taste	less	
	thank	less	

Let's practise

List **synonyms** for:

1 smelly _____

2 happy _____

3 difficult _____

4 ugly _____

5 cold _____

6 hot _____

7 dirty _____

8 hungry _____

9 thirsty _____

10 lost _____

List **antonyms** for:

11 straight _____

12 clear _____

13 loud _____

14 quiet _____

15 deep _____

16 shallow _____

17 big _____

18 small _____

19 old _____

20 young _____

Have a go

Use some of your words from above to write two sentences.

My idea of heaven is to be _____

_____

My idea of hell is to be _____

_____

15: Verbs

This is easy: a verb is a 'doing' word, like I **shout** or we **cry**.

Examples

1   The simplest verbs to write are those like **I run**, **I jump**.
    But we say **I am jumping** if the action goes on for some time.
2   You often have to change the verb for different people:
    I am thinking, but **you are** thinking, and **she is** thinking.
    We are thinking, **you are** thinking, **they are** thinking.
3   We call this the first, second and third person, either singular or plural:
    I am or **we are** is called the **first** person;
    you are is called the **second** person;
    he, **she**, **it is** or **they are** is called the **third** person.

	Singular	Plural
1st person	I	we
2nd person	you	you
3rd person	he, she, it	they

Get ready

1   What kinds of writing might be written in the first person?

_____

2   What kinds might be written in the second person?

_____

3   And what kinds might be written in the third person?

_____

Think of **verbs** to fill the gaps.

4 I _____ over the fence
and _____ on the ground.

5 The balloon _____ up into the sky and _____ away.

6 We are _____ing through the rain and _____ing in the puddles.

7 When it _____ it always _____ .

8 The cat _____ the mouse, who_____ under the bed.

Rewrite these in the **plural**, and say which person each is written in.

9 I always eat peas with honey. _____

10 I am thinking of going on holiday. _____

11 You always wash your car on Sunday. _____

12 He is coming for tea today. _____

13 It's sitting on the side. _____

Have a go

It is often said that a sentence isn't complete if it doesn't have a verb.
Which of these are real sentences? Underline the verbs.

14 Red sails in the sunset

15 Back to the future

16 I'm singing in the rain

17 The curious incident of the dog in the night-time

18 I'm getting married in the morning

19 The king and I

16: More on verbs

We've said that verbs change for different people. They also change for different *times*, which we call **tenses**: present, past and future.

Examples

Present: I **am** happy today, I **smile** or I **am smiling**.
Past: I **was** happy last week, I **smiled** or I **was smiling**.
Future: I **will be** happy next year, and I **will be smiling**.
When you add these endings to verbs, remember your spelling rules!

	Root word	**-ing** *ending*	**-ed** *ending*
Short vowel, followed by two consonants	stamp	stamping	stamped
Short vowel, followed by one consonant	bat	batting	batted
Long vowel sound	bark	barking	barked
Magic **e** *word*	hate	hating	hated
Ending in **y**	cry	crying	cried

Get ready

Write out the **-ing** and **-ed** endings for these verbs:

1 park _____

2 love _____

3 thank _____

4 fit _____

5 bury _____

Let's practise

Rewrite these sentences in the **past tense**:

6   I always eat peas with honey. _____

7   I am thinking of going on holiday. _____

8   He is coming for tea today. _____

9   It's sitting on the side. _____

Now rewrite them all in the **future tense**:

10 _____

11 _____

12 _____

13 _____

Have a go

There are lots of verbs that change totally in the past tense.
They tend to be the verbs we use most often. Can you fill in the boxes?

Present tense	Past tense
buy, think, catch, teach	bought, thought, caught, taught
	blew, grew, knew
keep, sweep, meet, lead	
	hung, sang, sank, stung
hide, slide	
	rode, strode, spoke
swim, run	
	found, bound

17: Pronouns

You remember we learnt about first, second and third person, with words like **I**, **you** and **he**, in Unit 15?

Those words are **pronouns**: pronouns stand in the place of complete nouns.

Examples

1   A pronoun can be the **subject** of a sentence, which means it's the person *who does* the verb:
    The king and **I** approached the queen.
    or **He** and **I** approached the queen.

2   A pronoun can be the **object** of a sentence, which means it's the person the verb is *done to*:
    The queen approached the king and **me**.
    or The queen approached **him** and **me**.

3   Or a pronoun can describe ownership: it's **mine**, or **yours**, or **his**. These are **possessive pronouns**. They never have an apostrophe. The words **my**, **your** or **her**, etc. are called **possessive adjectives**, not pronouns.

Can you fill the gaps in this grid?

	Singular subject	Singular object	Plural subject	Plural object
1st person	I	me	we	
2nd person	you		you	you
3rd person	he, she, it	him, her, it		them

1 Replace these nouns with **pronouns**.

The king invited **the queen** for tea. _____

The queen asked for **the honey**. _____

The knives were dirty. _____

The servants washed **the knives**. _____

Then **the courtiers** all sat down for **tea**. _____

2 Fill the gaps below with these words:

my, **your**, **her**, **their**, **our**, **yours**, **theirs**, **hers**, **his**, **its**

There are several choices; but everyone is talking about their own house.

I think that _____ house is smaller than _____ .

You said that _____ house was bigger than _____ house.

She said that _____ house had an oak tree in _____ garden.

They both said that _____ house was grander than _____ .

You and I know that _____ house is better than _____ .

 Finally, see if you can fill the gaps in this grid.

	Singular possessive adjective	Singular possessive pronoun	Plural possessive adjective	Plural possessive pronoun
1st person	my	mine	our	ours
2nd person	your	yours	your	
3rd person	his, her, its	his, hers		theirs

18: Adverbs

An **adverb** describes a verb, like he sang **loudly**.

Examples

1   Adverbs, like adjectives, can make your writing more interesting:
    He replied **rapidly**.
    She replied **carefully**.
    The audience responded **favourably**.

2   You can put adverbs in different places to give different effects:
    Angrily she left the room.
    She stalked **angrily** from the room.
    She left the room **angrily**.

3   When you compare adverbs, you usually need two words:
    I can see **clearly**, you see **more clearly**, but he sees **most clearly** of all.
    She ran **quickly**, I ran **more quickly**, but you ran **most quickly** of all.
    But I did **well**, you did **better**, and she did **best** of all.

4   Some words can be either adjectives or adverbs:
    The **fast** (adjective) car drove **fast** (adverb) round the bend.
    The **better** (adjective) child did **better** (adverb) at school.

Turn these adjectives into adverbs – and remember the spelling rules.

Root adjective	Adverb with -ly ending
plain	plainly
dark	
pale	
late	
blunt	
fitful	
merry	

Let's practise

Fill in **adverbs** to make these sentences into a story:

I arrived _____. She opened the door _____.
We talked _____. She left the room _____.
I left the house _____.

Fill the gaps with **comparative** or **superlative** adverbs:

1   I count cleverly, but he counts _____.

2   You paint brilliantly, but I paint _____.

3   I jump high, but they jump _____.

4   They run fast, but we run _____.

5   I bought more than she did, but she bought _____.

Have a go

Some adverbs don't end in **-ly**.
These are often adverbs of **time**, **place** or **manner**. For example:

Now and **then** I look **around**.
Soon I will **only** want to run **away**.

You can sometimes use adverbs like this to structure an argument.

Try completing these sentences to express your point of view about something:

First I want to state my opinion that _____
Next I want to suggest that _____
However you may be thinking that _____
Whereas I reckon that _____
Therefore I conclude that _____

How have I done?

SPELLING

1 Plurals

Lots of (donkey) _____, (monkey) _____ and (husky) _____.

Heaps of (tomato) _____, (marrow) _____ and (potato) _____.

Bags of (leaf) _____, (scarf) _____ and (loaf) _____.

Tons of (box) _____, (dress) _____ and (watch) _____.

2 Word endings

The dog sat on the (mating/matting) _____ and (barcked/barked) _____ (noisily/noisyly) _____ until the (angry/angrey) _____ neighbours (told/tolled) _____ it to be (quiet/quite) _____.

3 -ight or -ite

Let's l_____ the fire.

She m_____ come with you.

Give me a b_____ of your apple.

You gave me a fr_____!

The snow is wh_____r than wh_____.

Let's f_____ the good f_____ with all our m_____.

4 -tion or -sion

The train leaves the sta_____ .

Don't even men_____ it.

Stand to atten_____ .

The book is a new ver_____ of the old edi_____.

My deci_____ is final.

In maths we do addi_____, subtrac_____, multiplica_____ and divi_____.

⑤ Apostrophes

I (shant) _____ say what (youve) _____ just said.

I (cant) _____ repeat what (hes) _____ told me.

The (childrens) _____ ball fell off (its) _____ shelf and landed
   on the two (boys) _____ feet.

That poor (donkeys) _____ ears are shorter than all those other
   (donkeys) _____ ears.

The (wives) _____ hats blew off in the (winds) _____ path.

GRAMMAR

Put the numbers in the texts against the right parts of speech:

⑥ Parts of speech

At the end[1] of the day, the best[2] person will win[3] the place that he or she[4]
deserves, on their[5] merit, and they will triumph magnificently[6]!

Adjective _____   Noun _____   Pronoun _____

Adverb_____   Possessive adjective _____   Verb _____

⑦ Same again!

At the end of the day[1], the best person[2] will win the place[3] that he or she
deserves[4], on their merit[5], and they[6] will triumph magnificently!

Adjective _____   Noun _____   Pronoun _____

Adverb_____   Possessive adjective _____   Verb _____

⑧ What kind of pronouns?

If we[1] put my[2] cash with yours[3], then our[4] savings are bigger than theirs[5].

Pronoun _____   Possessive adjective _____   Possessive pronoun _____

⑨ Adjective or adverb?

The fast[1] car drove fast[2] round the tight[3] bend and nearly[4] swept the
frightened[5] pedestrian off the drenched[6] pavement.

Adjective _____   Adverb _____

Answers

UNIT 1
Let's practise
1 bunches 2 boxes 3 volcanoes 4 dishes 5 potatoes
6 messes 7 dinosaurs 8 envelopes 9 classes 10 gloves
11 fairies 12 dwarves 13 diaries 14 children 15 donkeys
16 men 17 cowboys 18 knives 19 jellies 20 calves

Have a go
swarm, flock, school

UNIT 2
1 jump 2 quick 3 hope 4 wash 5 like 6 greenhouse 7 airport
8 playground 9 haircut 10 cardboard 11 saucepan or
sauceboat 12 sunshine or moonshine 13 teacup or eggcup
14 eyebrow or eyelash or eyelid 15 toenail

UNIT 3
1

Prefix	Root word	New word	Meaning
un	able	unable	cannot do
	common	uncommon	rare
	true	untrue	false
	usual	unusual	uncommon
	even	uneven	rough
pre	historic	prehistoric	ancient
	view	preview	look at before
re	fresh	refresh	clean up
	fund	refund	give back
	cycle	recycle	use again

2

Root word	Suffix	New word	Meaning
pain	ful	painful	hurts a lot
power	ful	powerful	important
meaning	ful	meaningful	lot of sense
plate	ful	plateful	full plate
pain	less	painless	no pain
spot	less	spotless	no spots!
life	less	lifeless	dead
walk	able	walkable	can be walked
bear	able	bearable	can be put up with
suit	able	suitable	appropriate

UNIT 4
Get ready

If you want to find out	You ask
The date or time	When?
The reason	Why?
The place	Where?
Which person	Who?
Who it belongs to	Whose?
What it is	What?
Which particular thing	Which?

Let's practise

Silent letter	Spelling	Meaning
w	wreck	old ship
	wrist	between hand and arm
	wren	very small bird
	wrong	not right
	wrinkle	small furrow
k	knock	hit
	knight	man in armour
	knit	make with wool
	knife	tool for cutting
g	gnarled	bent and twisted
	gnaw	chew

Have a go
Sample answers:
What is your earliest memory? When did it happen? Where
did it happen? Who do you remember? Whose family was it?
Which time of year? Why do you remember it?

UNIT 5
Get ready

Short vowel	Add magic **e**
fin	fine
spit	spite
fat	fate
cub	cube
mop	mope
can	cane
hop	hope
dam	dame
bit	bite
shin	shine
rob	robe
spin	spine

Let's practise
Short: hit, bank, fond, fin, pun
Long: moon, lie, stay, feet, moan
Magic **e**: phone, plate, line, fate, pole

Have a go
To run is fun
To race is ace
To shine is fine
To care is rare

UNIT 6
Get ready

bat	met	fin	hot	mug
chat	bet	shin	plot	bug
that	get	chin	shot	hug
flat	let	thin	blot	plug

Let's practise
Short vowel

word	Add **-ing**	Add **-ed**	Add **-er**
flip	flipping	flipped	flipper
stop	stopping	stopped	stopper
fold	folding	folded	folder
pat	patting	patted	patter
pop	popping	popped	popper
ban	banning	banned	banner
slip	slipping	slipped	slipper
pot	potting	potted	potter
mist	misting	misted	mister
chat	chatting	chatted	chatter
thin	thinning	thinned	thinner

Have a go

Short vowel	*Long vowel*
tinny	tiny
dinner	diner
matting	mating
pinning	pining
fussing	fusing
matted	mated
fatted	fated
stripped	striped

UNIT 7
Get ready

Root word	**-ing** *ending*	**-ed** *ending*
fry	frying	fried
try	trying	tried
cry	crying	cried
die	dying	died
lie	lying	lied
tie	tying	tied

Let's practise

Root word	**-ing** *ending*	**-y** *ending*	**-ed** *ending*
squeak	squeaking	squeaky	squeaked
float	floating	floaty	floated
brood	brooding	broody	brooded
sneak	sneaking	sneaky	sneaked
rain	raining	rainy	rained
need	needing	needy	needed
flake	flaking	flaky	flaked
pose	posing	posy	posed
stone	stoning	stony	stoned
phone	phoning	phony	phoned
taste	tasting	tasty	tasted
bone	boning	bony	boned
paste	pasting	pasty	pasted

Have a go
1 **ar** as in spark, bark, park, hard, tart, etc.
2 **aw** as in bawdy, raw, lawn, saw, etc.
3 **oi** as in moist, coin, boil, etc.
4 **ou** as in house, mouth, mouse, etc.
5 **ow** as in rowdy, cow, town, etc.

UNIT 8
Examples

-ttle	**-ddle**	**-zzle**	**-bble**	**-ffle**
little	puddle	drizzle	bubble	raffle
bottle	muddle	puzzle	pebble	skiffle
skittle	middle	fizzle	dribble	shuffle
table	**ea**gle	s**ti**fle	r**u**ble	
cable	treacle	Bible	bugle	
fable	people	rifle	doodle	
stable	needle	trifle	poodle	

Get ready
In the middle of the drizzle,
While we're shuffling through the puddles,
Let's keep blowing bubbles
Till the drizzle is a dribble!

Let's practise
Short vowel followed by two consonants: jumble, jungle,
     scramble, trickle
Short vowel followed by a double consonant: muffle, piffle,
     giggle, juggle
Long vowel sound: dawdle, marble, bauble, cradle

-al *endings*	**-el** *endings*
final	easel
tribal	label
legal	hazel
oval	tunnel
global	funnel
focal	weasel
local	model
equal	rebel
metal	level
fatal etc.	camel etc.

UNIT 9
Get ready
1 bright, radiant
2 fight, attack
3 flight, flying
4 fright, fear
5 knight, man in armour
6 light, not dark
7 night, not day
8 right, correct
9 sight, seeing
10 tight, not loose

Let's practise

'ow(t)' sound	*'off' sound*	*'oh' sound*	*'oo' sound*	*'ort' sound*	*'uh' sound*	*'uff' sound*
bough	cough	though	through	thought	thorough	tough
plough	trough	although		nought	borough	rough
drought		dough		fought		enough
				sought		
				bought		

Have a go

'arf' sound	'ay' sound	'ite' sound	'ort' sound
laugh	eight	height	naughty
	weight		daughter
	sleigh		slaughter
	straight		caught

UNIT 10
Let's practise
1 **able**: printable, reliable, readable, valuable
2 **ible**: edible, flexible, legible, visible
3 **tion**: caption, emotion, fiction, option
4 **sion**: division, pension, mansion, revision

Have a go
ssion: fission, session, emission, omission, etc.
shion: cushion, fashion, etc.

UNIT 11
Get ready

Full	Short	Cut
she is	she's	i
I have	I've	ha
we had	we'd	ha
we are	we're	a
they have	they've	ha
do not	don't	o
cannot	can't	no
it is	it's	i
who is	who's	i
should not	shouldn't	o
must not	mustn't	o

Let's practise
1 The queen's crown
2 The queen's crowns
3 The queens' crowns
4 The boys' football
5 The camel's humps
6 The soldier's leg
7 The grannies' house
8 The grannies' houses

Have a go
9 The children's legs
10 The children's toy
11 The men's trousers
12 The ladies' shoes

UNIT 12
Let's practise
6 I would like to know which wood you mean.
7 Let's make our peace with a piece of cake.
8 I knew you had new socks on.
9 Which way did the witch go?
10 They're saying that they live there.
11 I think the sum will take some time.
12 I reckon two pieces is too few.
13 No doubt you know the answer.
14 This hole is a whole lot harder to dig.
15 Where did you wear this coat before?

Have a go
16 I know that it's not always easy to know if it's right.
17 But its meaning should be as clear as it's always been.
18 It's just a question of checking what it's meant to mean.
19 On its own, it's never a problem.
20 But it's right to feel perplexed about how it's used.

UNIT 13
Let's practise

Adjective	Comparative	Superlative
dark	darker	darkest
deep	deeper	deepest
plain	plainer	plainest
pale	paler	palest
stale	staler	stalest
tasty	tastier	tastiest
red	redder	reddest
dim	dimmer	dimmest
thin	thinner	thinnest
fit	fitter	fittest
batty	battier	battiest

Have a go

Noun	Adjective
rose	rosy
friend	friendly
book	bookish
care	careful

UNIT 14
Get ready
Antonyms: unclear, defrost, disagree, distrust, dishonest, impossible, impolite, hopeless, tasteless, thankless

UNIT 15
1 Diaries, letters, autobiography, recounts, discussions
2 Instructions, directions, explanations, persuasion
3 Narrative, reports, recounts, biography

Let's practise
9 We always eat peas with honey. (First person)
10 We are thinking of going on holiday. (First person)
11 You always wash your cars on Sunday. (Second person)
12 They are coming for tea today. (Third person)
13 They are sitting on the side. (Third person)

Have a go
14 No verb
15 No verb
16 I'm singing in the rain.
17 No verb
18 I'm getting married in the morning.
19 No verb

UNIT 16
Get ready
1 park, parking, parked
2 love, loving, loved
3 thank, thanking, thanked
4 fit, fitting, fitted
5 bury, burying, buried

Let's practise
6 I always ate peas with honey.
7 I was thinking of going on holiday.
8 He was coming for tea today.
9 It was sitting on the side.

10 I shall/will always eat peas with honey.
11 I shall/will be thinking of going on holiday.
12 He will be coming for tea today.
13 It will be sitting on the side.

Have a go

Present tense	Past tense
buy, think, catch, teach	bought, thought, caught, taught
blow, grow, know	blew, grew, knew
keep, sweep, meet, lead	kept, swept, met, led
hang, sing, sink, sting	hung, sang, sank, stung
hide, slide	hid, slid
ride, stride, speak	rode, strode, spoke
swim, run	swam, ran
find, bind	found, bound

UNIT 17
Get ready

	Singular subject	Singular object	Plural subject	Plural object
1st person	I	me	we	us
2nd person	you	you	you	you
3rd person	he, she, it	him, her, it	they	them

Let's practise

1 **He** invited **her** for tea.
   She asked for **it**.
   They were dirty.
   They washed **them**.
   Then **they** all sat down for **it**.

2 I think that my house is smaller than yours/his/hers/theirs.
   You said that your house was bigger than my/his/her/our/their house.
   She said that her house had an oak tree in its garden.
   They both said that their house was grander than mine/yours/his/hers/ours.
   You and I know that our house is better than his/hers/theirs.

Have a go

	Singular possessive adjective	Singular possessive pronoun	Plural possessive adjective	Plural possessive pronoun
1st person	my	mine	our	ours
2nd person	your	yours	your	yours
3rd person	his, her, its	his, hers	their	theirs

UNIT 18
Get ready

Root adjective	Adverb with **-ly** ending
plain	plainly
dark	darkly
pale	palely
late	lately
blunt	bluntly
fitful	fitfully
merry	merrily

Let's practise

1 I count cleverly, but he counts more/most cleverly.
2 You paint brilliantly, but I paint more/most brilliantly.
3 I jump high, but they jump higher/highest.
4 They run fast, but we run faster/fastest.
5 I bought more, but she bought most.

How have I done? – Spelling
1 Plurals
Lots of donkeys, monkeys and huskies.
Heaps of tomatoes, marrows and potatoes.
Bags of leaves, scarves and loaves.
Tons of boxes, dresses and watches.

2 Word endings
The dog sat on the matting and barked noisily until the angry neighbours told it to be quiet.

3 -ight or -ite
Let's light the fire.
She might come with you.
Give me a bite of your apple.
You gave me a fright!
The snow is whiter than white.
Let's fight the good fight with all our might.

4 -tion or -sion
The train leaves the station.
Don't even mention it.
Stand to attention.
The book is a new version of the old edition.
My decision is final.
In maths we do addition, subtraction, multiplication and division.

5 Apostrophes
I shan't say what you've just said.
I can't repeat what he's told me.
The children's ball fell off its shelf and landed on the two boys' feet.
That poor donkey's ears are shorter than all those other donkeys' ears.
The wives' hats blew off in the wind's path.

Grammar
6 Parts of speech
Adjective 2
Noun 1
Pronoun 4
Adverb 6
Possessive adjective 5
Verb 3

7 Same again!
Noun 1, 2, 3, 5
Pronoun 6
Verb 4

8 What kind of pronouns?
Pronoun 1
Possessive adjective 2, 4
Possessive pronoun 3, 5

9 Adjective or adverb?
Adjective 1, 3, 5, 6
Adverb 2, 4

Spelling poem

Spelling nightmare!

We've made our lists of spellings now,
Of **tough** and **dough** and **rough** and **bough**;
So now it's up to none but you
To master **thorough**, **cough** and **through**.
Well done! You've also learned perhaps
Of other earlier fearful traps.

Beware of **heard**, a dreadful word
That looks like **beard** and sounds like **bird**;
And **dead**, it's said like **bed** not **bead**.
For goodness' sake don't call it **deed**!
Watch out for **meat** and **great** and **threat**:
They rhyme with **suite** and **straight** and **debt**.

A **moth** is not the moth in **mother**,
Nor **both** in **bother** or **broth** in **brother**.
And **here** is not a match for **there**,
Nor **dear** or **fear** or **peer** for **bear**.
And then there's **dose** and **rose** and **lose**,
But double o for **goose** and **choose**.

There's **cork** and **work**, and **card** and **ward**,
And **font** and **front**, and **word** and **sword**.
There's **do** and **go**, and **thwart** and **cart**.
Hang on, I've hardly made a start!
A tricky language, yours and mine:
You'd best begin before you're nine!